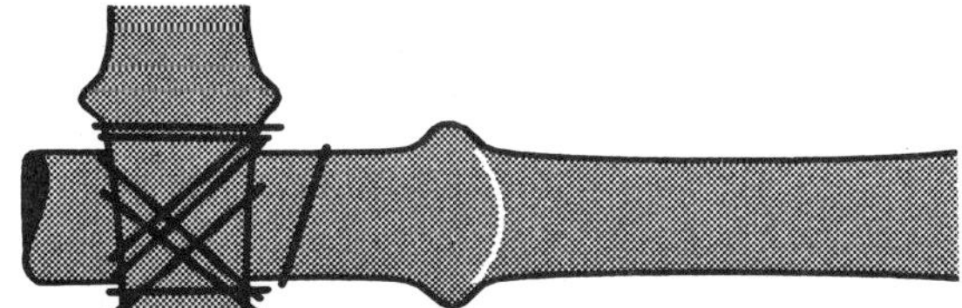

China

Components

Folktale: The unit begins with a folktale that serves as a springboard for the cross-curricular activities. The story can be read at several points in the unit -- to introduce the unit, before or after the Pocket Chart Activity, and in conjunction with the Story Mat.

Folktale Follow-Up: Questions in the Folktale Follow-Up enable children to discover some of the unique aspects and customs of the culture. Through the story and the illustrations, children become aware of such topics as dress, food, language, and housing.

Pocket Chart Strips and Activities: A portion of the story that lends itself to chanting has been rendered on pocket chart strips. Whole language suggestions are included. Children can learn the chant before or after reading the story; once they know the chant, they can join in wholeheartedly on the storytelling.

Story Mat and Characters: After cutting out and assembling the story characters, children can use them on the Story Mat as the folktale is being told. The Story Mat is also a useful vehicle for encouraging groups of children to act out the folktale.

Activities and Blackline Masters: A set of hands-on activities are included to expand children's awareness of the culture. Developed with the idea of integrating all parts of the curriculum, the activities incorporate:

foreign language	math	science	dress
cooking	creative arts	drama	dance
music	creative writing	language arts	

Each activity is divided into the following sections for easy use:

- Cultural background
- Preparation
- Activity and Blackline Master

Additional Literature: A current bibliography of children's literature related to the culture is provided.

Glossary: The glossary includes foreign language words used throughout the unit. The pronunciation key is as follows:

a as in father	ah	o as in wrote	oh
a as in sap	a	u as in flute	oo
e as in feed	ee	u as in hurt	u
e as in bed	eh		

Children and Families as Resources: Whenever possible, encourage the children in your classroom who are familiar with the culture to share their knowledge and insights, and invite their families to enrich the program.

Congratulations on your purchase of some of the finest teaching materials in the world.

Table of Contents

Our Philosophy

The world is a smaller place these days, and children in our classrooms are from many cultures. This series offers stepping stones toward the goal of mutual respect among children of different backgrounds. The program offers an integrated curriculum, with whole class, cooperative group, and individual activities for the primary grades. Interviews were the primary source of information, giving the hands-on activities their authenticity, detail, and interest.

A special thank you to Alice Chen, Lily Chin, and Kitty Pang
for their invaluable contributions to this book.

The Terrible Dragon

Retold by Betsy Franco

Chinese Words in the Story:

lyong (lyohng)—dragon
fan (fahn)— cooked rice
Ni hao ma (nee how mah)—How are you?

A long time ago in a small village in China, there was a terrible dragon. No one had ever actually seen the dragon, but all parents warned their children, "If you are naughty, the terrible lyong will wake up in his cave! He'll fly to our house and carry you away! This terrible dragon has the scaly long body of a snake and the bulging eyeballs of a shrimp. He has the beard of a man, the paws of a tiger, and the toes of an eagle."

The children of the village were very frightened, especially when they had been naughty. But there was one small boy in the village who was never frightened of anything. His name was Wen Li.

Wen Li was not afraid of the terrible dragon. He wasn't even sure he believed the dragon story. Also, Wen Li was hardly ever naughty. When the dragon was brought up, he would say,

"To tell the truth, I'm not afraid
of dragons living in a cave.
And when I meet one face-to-face,
I know for sure that I'll be brave."

Wen Li was almost ten years old. In China, living ten years called for a celebration. So Wen Li's parents were planning a birthday party.

"When you are inviting people," Wen Li said to his parents, "I would like one special guest."

"Who is that?" asked Wen Li's mother.

"I would like to invite the terrible dragon," said Wen Li, "I have never seen him, and I would like to meet him."

His parents protested, "That's impossible, Wen Li. No one has ever seen the terrible dragon."

"There's no way to find him!" Wen Li's father said firmly.

But this did not stop Wen Li. The next day, his mother packed him a box lunch of steamed fan with salted cabbage and sent him off to play. With his lunch under his arm, Wen Li headed for the hills surrounding the village.

“There must be a cave here somewhere,” he thought.

Sure enough, over the next hill, he came upon the mouth of a cave, covered with spider webs. Wen Li put down his box lunch and said to himself,

> "To tell the truth, I'm not afraid
> of dragons living in a cave.
> And when I meet one face-to-face,
> I know for sure that I'll be brave."

Then he leaned down toward the opening of the cave and called, "Yoo-hoo. Is anyone there? Ni hao ma?"

Wen Li heard sounds from deep in the cave. Rumble. Thump. Thump. Thump. The sound drew closer, and suddenly the opening of the cave was filled by a terrible dragon with a scaly long body of a snake and the eyeballs of a shrimp. He had the beard of a man, the paws of a tiger, and the toes of an eagle.

Wen Li was startled, but he stayed right where he was. He said to himself,

"To tell the truth, I'm not afraid
of dragons living in a cave.
And when I meet one face-to-face,
I know for sure that I'll be brave."

The dragon moved back a step and bowed his head. In a very small, frightened voice, he said, "What do you want?"

"I'm having a birthday party," said Wen Li, "and I'd like to invite you." Wen Li noticed that the dragon's scales were dusty and his claws were chipped and dirty.

The dragon couldn't believe his ears, "What are you saying?" he said in a very gentle voice.

"You're invited to my birthday party," Wen Li repeated. He noticed that the dragon's beard needed combing. Then he saw giant tears forming in the dragon's eyes and landing on the ground.

"Why are you crying?" Wen Li asked.

"In all my days living in a cave, no one has ever been kind to me," said the dragon. "I would love to go to your birthday party. Hop on my back and I will take you home."

Wen Li leaped onto the dragon's back. He looked down and saw that the dragon's tears had turned into a river. Down the river floated Wen Li perched on the dragon.

When they reached the village, everyone ran to hide.

"The dragon has come! He has captured Wen Li!" they cried.

But one by one, they noticed that Wen Li was smiling and that the dragon was actually a dragon boat powered by steam. The dragon had turned into a boat, and Wen Li was the dragon boat captain.

People came from all around to celebrate Wen Li's tenth birthday on board the dragon boat. At the dragon boat festival that year, Wen Li had the largest, most beautiful boat of all.

From that day on, Wen Li was greatly respected throughout the village. When he passed by, people would remember his adventure and say to one another, "One kindness always pays off in another kindness."

Folktale Follow-Up

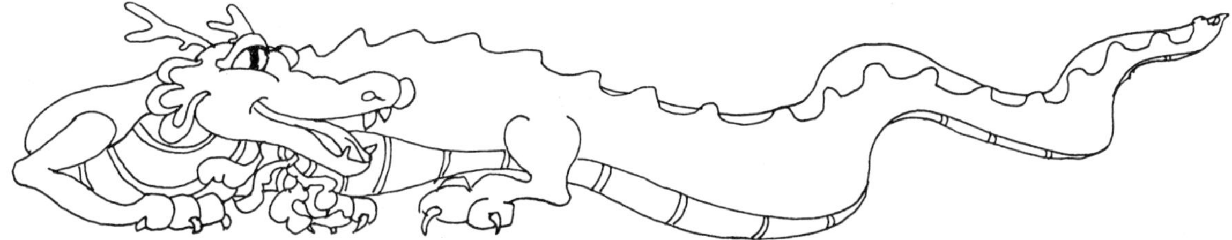

1. What do you notice about the way the characters are dressed?

Wen Li is wearing an outfit consisting of wide-legged cotton pants and a high-collared jacket with buttons down the middle. Wen Li's father has on a similar outfit. His mother is wearing the same type of pants but her jacket has Chinese buttons starting in the middle and moving toward the right and down the side. Today, some people in the villages still wear these traditional Chinese work clothes. In the cities, people can also be seen in western clothes, such as blue jeans.

2. Share some things about a Chinese house.

We do not see Wen Li's house in the story. It would probably have been made of mud and covered by a thatched, pointed roof. Inside there would be one room. One corner would be for sleeping. The beds would be platforms covered with straw mats and quilts. The cooking area and the bathroom would be outside the house. In China today, some people still live in mud homes. In cities, people live in small apartments.

3. What can you say about Chinese food from the story?

Wen Li's mother packed him a lunch of steamed fan (rice) with salted cabbage to make it taste good. Rice is eaten at every meal. It is a staple food in China. Vegetables, such as cabbage, onions, mushrooms, squash, and leafy greens, are commonly eaten as well. Today, the diet also includes fish, eggs, and some meat, such as chicken and pork.

Other ways to use
The Terrible Dragon

• Reproduce the story several times. Staple each copy inside a cover. Send the copies home with different children each night until all students have had an opportunity to share the story with their family. You may want parents to write a comment on the back cover explaining how their family shared the book and how they felt about it.

• If your students are at a level where they can read the story themselves, reproduce several copies for children to use for shared reading.

• Once your students are familiar with the story, reproduce the pictures on page 19. Have children cut the pictures apart and put them in the sequence they occur in the story. The pictures can then be used to...

1. Paste the story in order onto a large sheet of paper. (Have children refer to the original story if they have difficulty with the order.)

2. Create a picture book.
    - Paste the pictures into a book.
    - Use the pictures as you retell the story to a friend.

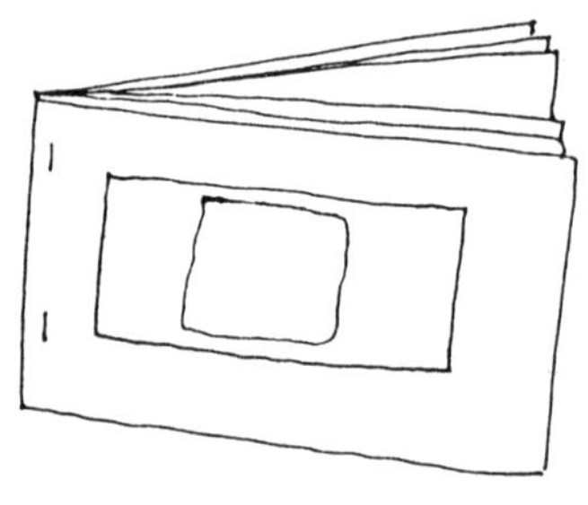

3. Rewrite the story.
    - Paste each picture to a sheet of writing paper.
    - Write about that part of the story.
    - Staple the finished pages together in order.
    - Make a cover for your book.

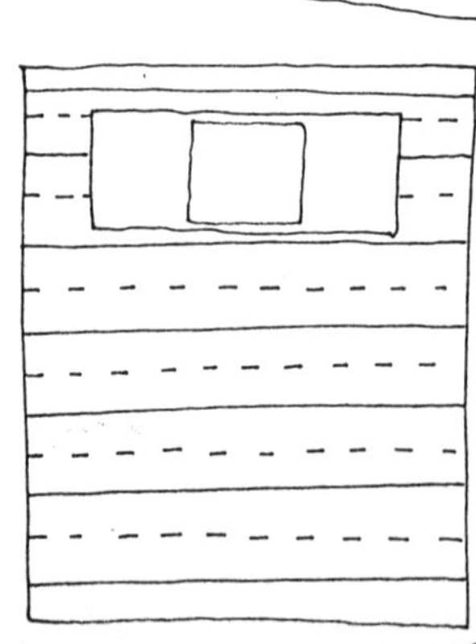

Note: Reproduce to use in retelling the story of ***The Terrible Dragon.***

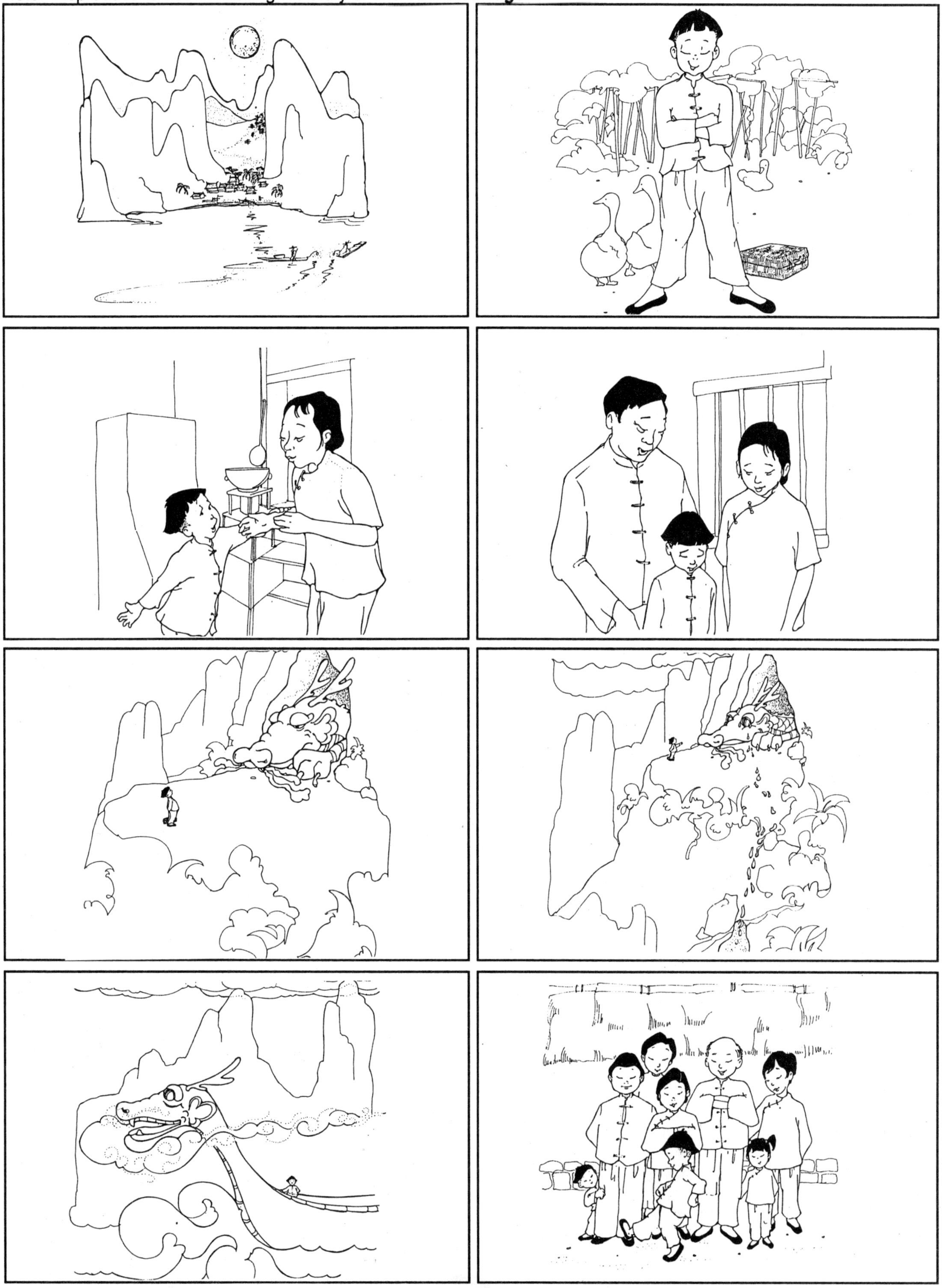

Pocket Chart Activity

Cut out the strips on pages 21-24 and place them in a pocket chart.

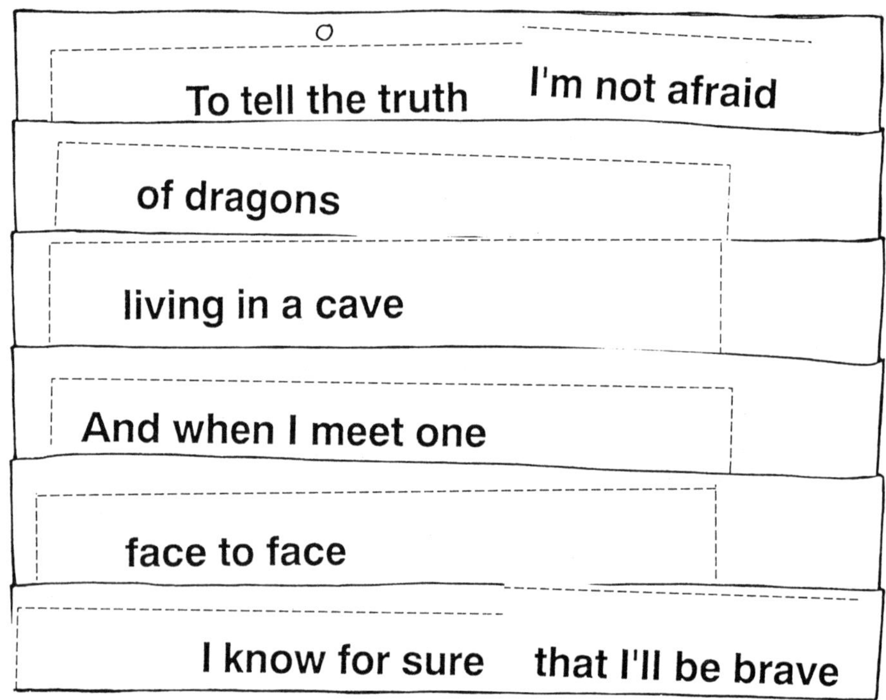

The chant can be read over and over again:

• It can be read after the first reading of the folktale and chanted over and over again, as it occurs in the story. Then in the second reading of the folktale, the children can join in on the verses.

• It can be read prior to the folktale.

Below are some suggestions for this particular chant:

• Have the children repeat the chant using different kinds of voices. (How would Wen Li have said the refrain when talking to his parents? How would he have said it at the mouth of the cave?)
• Let the children spot the rhyming words. Have them discover the similarity in the spellings of cave and brave. Encourage them to think of other words that rhyme with cave, (save, Dave, pave, wave, grave).
• Talk about the contractions in the chant—I'm and I'll—and let children explain what they stand for.
• Give the children a chance to complete the frame below, acknowledging fears they've overcome and times they've been brave. "To tell the truth, I used to be afraid (of, to) ______________________________ but now I'm not."

Pocket Chart Strips

To tell the truth

I'm not afraid

of dragons

living in a cave

And when I meet one

face-to-face

I know for sure

that I'll be brave

Characters

Put these characters on the Story Mat to act out the folktale as your teacher reads it, or act out the story in small groups.

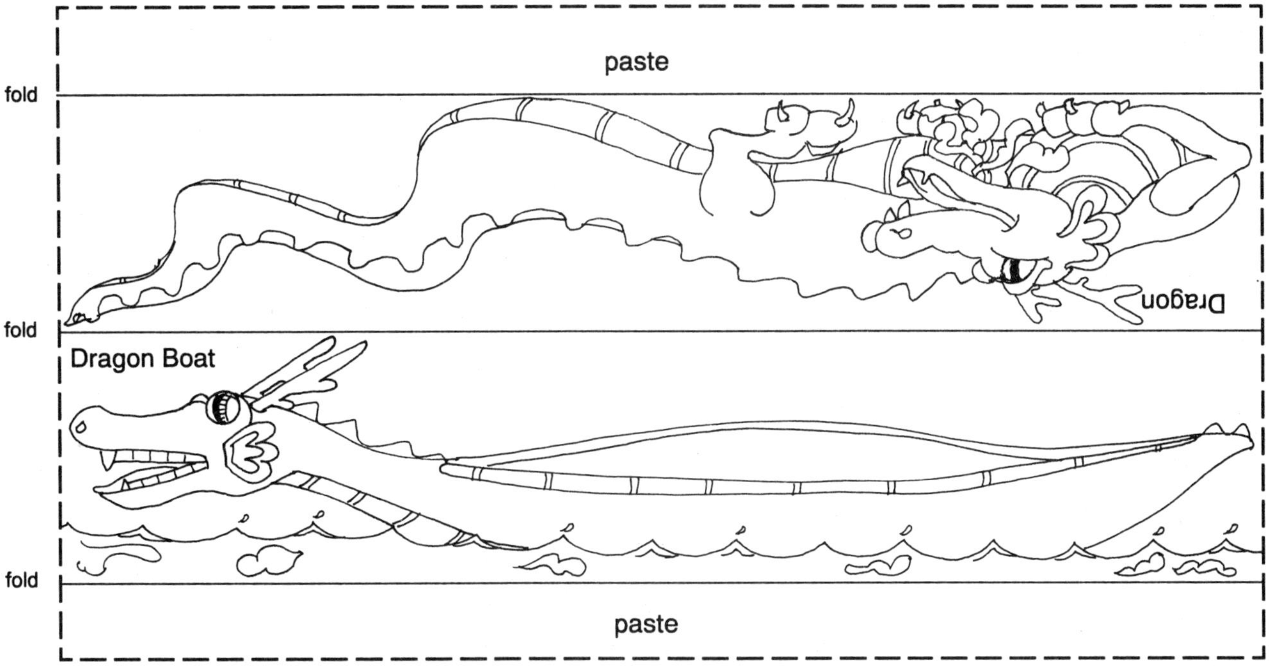

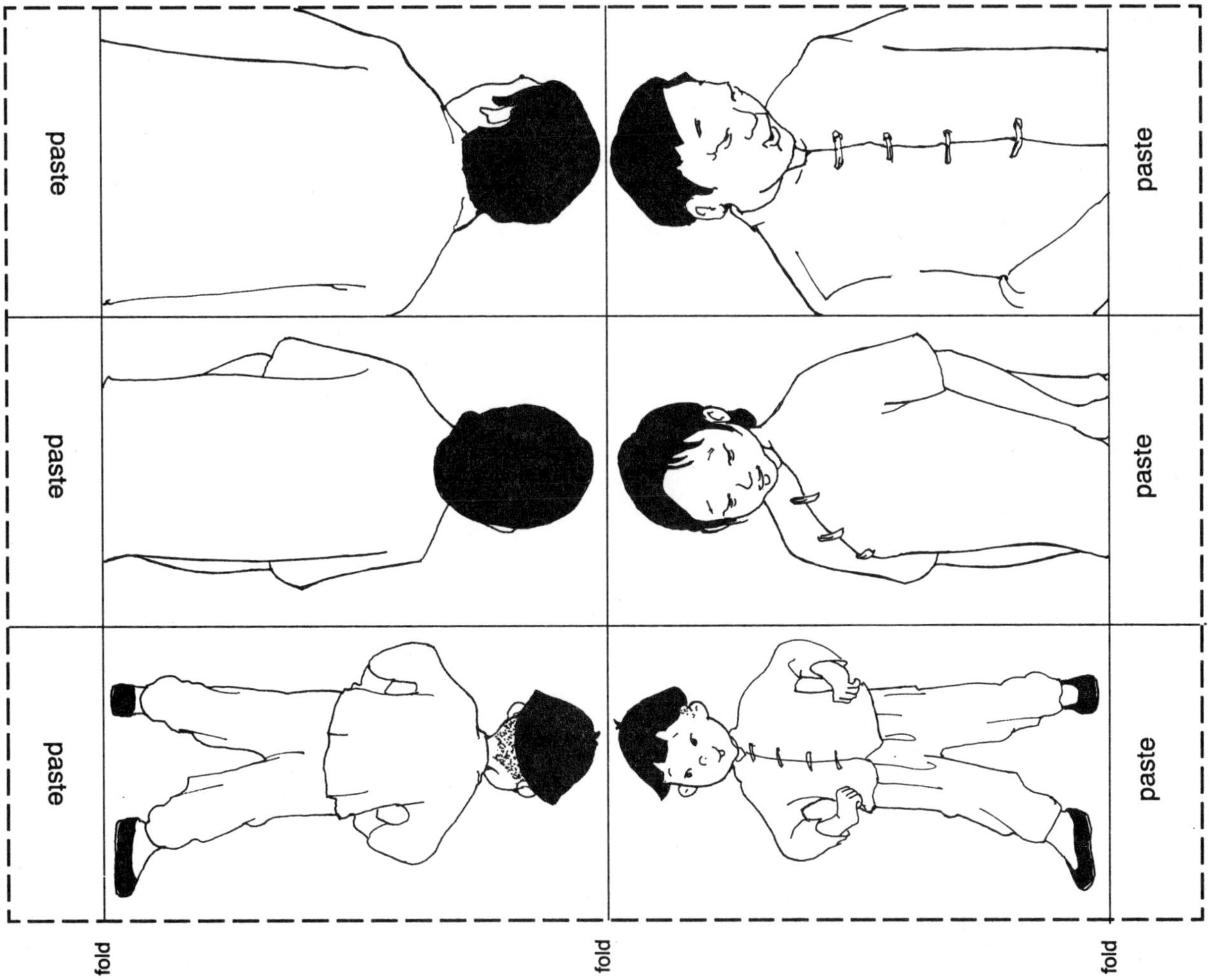

paste

fold

Dragon

fold

Dragon Boat

fold

paste

paste

paste

paste

paste

paste

paste

fold

fold

fold

Story Mat

paste to page 27

Story Mat continued.

Writing Chinese Words

Cultural Background

Chinese is a very musical language. The four tones in the spoken language are almost like musical notes on a scale. The same sound can have many different meanings depending on the tone—flat, rising, falling and rising, or falling. For example, below are two words pronounced "ma" (mah). Each has a different tone, a different meaning, and is represented by a different Chinese character.

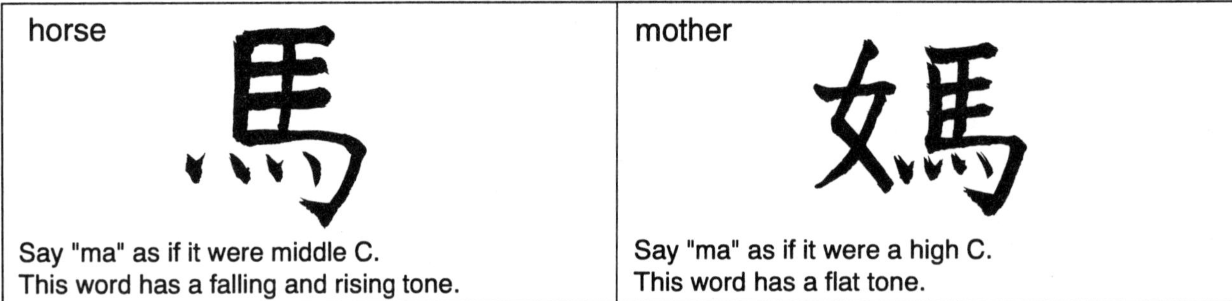

The Chinese written language is the oldest one in the world. It evolved from picture writing into the characters used today. The strokes for each Chinese characters are written in a particular direction and order.

Preparation

To write the Chinese characters, each child will need copies of pages 29 and 30.
You might want to practice each character before the lesson.

Activity

• Explain the difference between the sound for horse and the sound for mother.
• Have the children look at the characters on page 29. Discuss the similarity between the way the character looks and what it means. Have the children say the Mandarin Chinese words for each character, shown below:

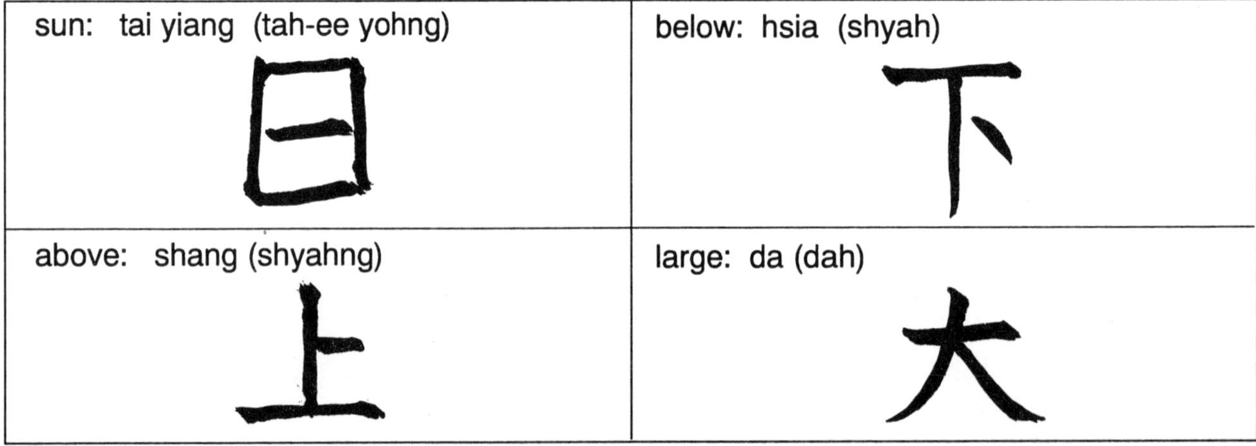

above: shang (shyahng) 上	**below: hsia (shyah)** 下
sun: tai yiang (tah-ee-yohng) 日	**large: da (dah)** 大

Writing Practice

above **shang (shyahng)**

丨	卜	上	上

below **hsia (shyah)**

一	丅	下	下

Writing Practice continued.

sun **tai yiang (tah-ee-yohng)**

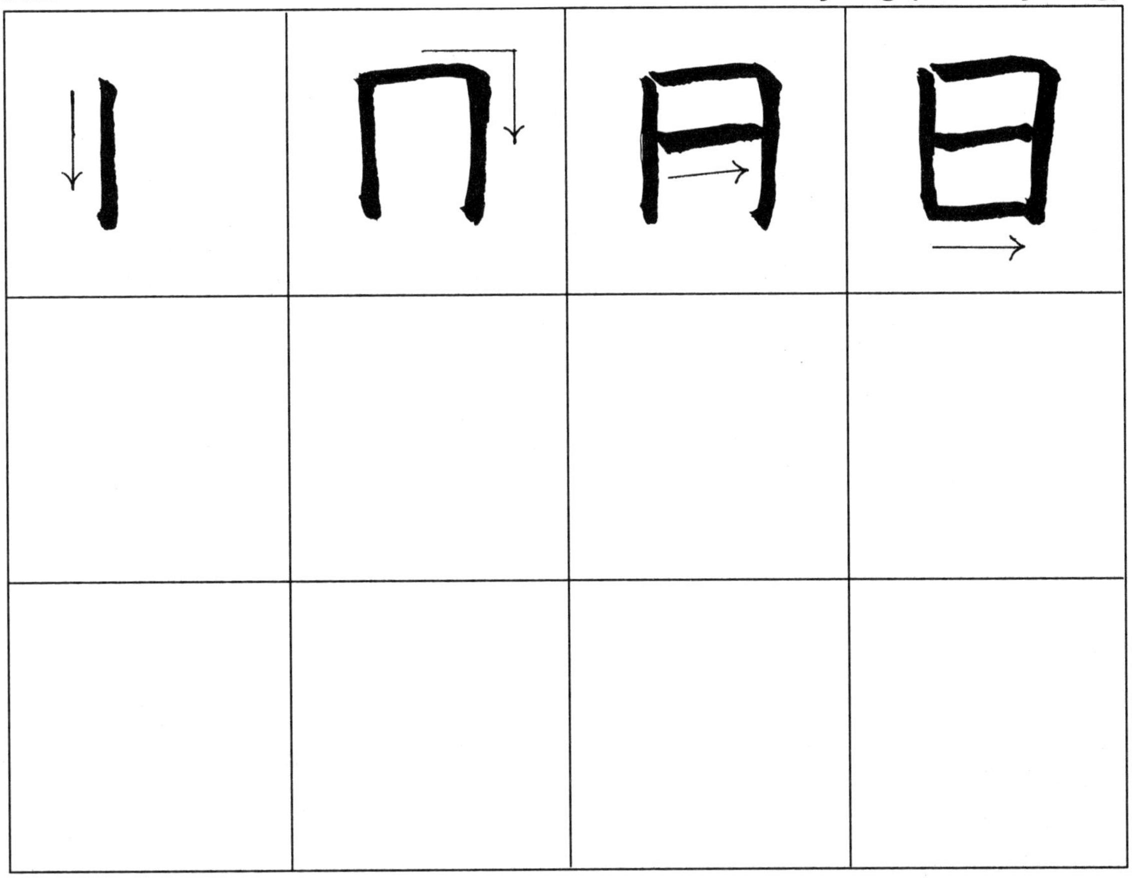

large **da (dah)**

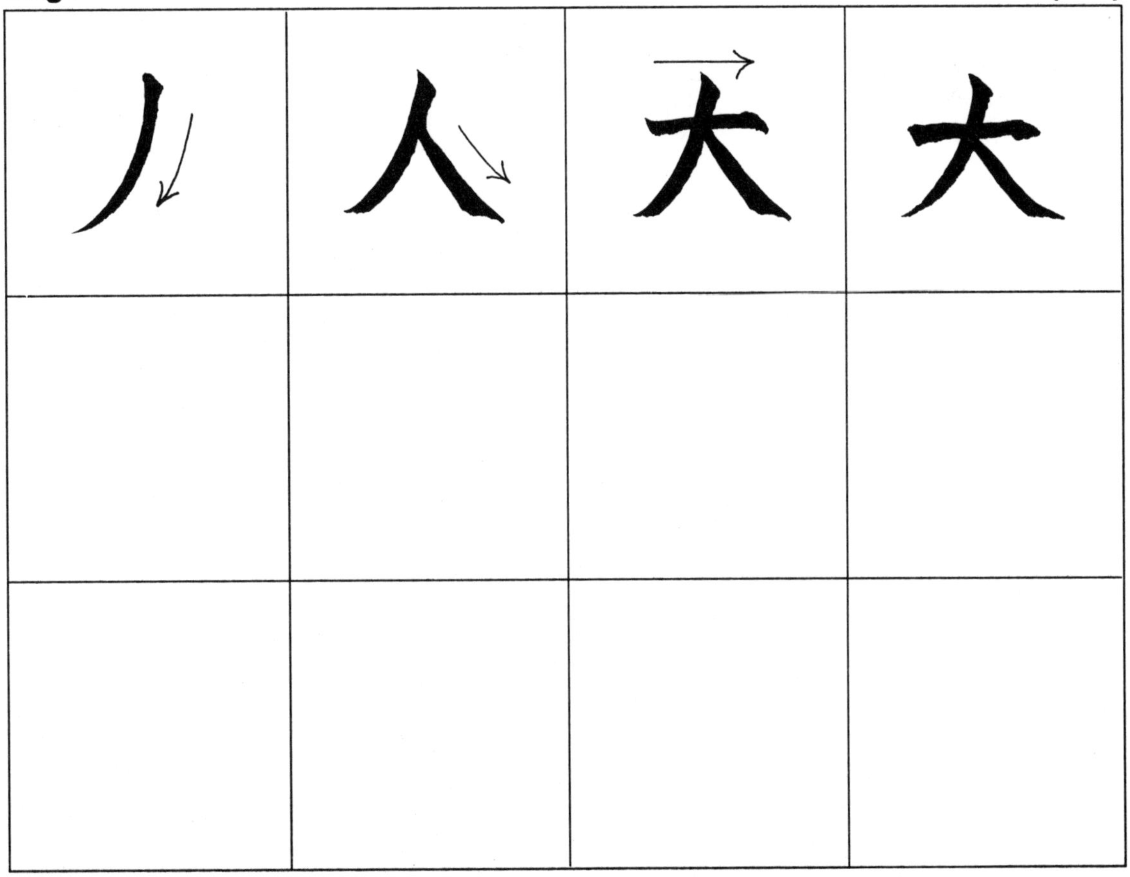

端午節

Celebrating the Dragon Boat Festival

Cultural Background

The Dragon Boat Festival, Duan Wu Jie (Dwahn woh JEE-eh), takes place on the fifth day of the fifth moon (around June 21). The festival is based on the belief that the dragon gods (serpents) control the rivers and the rainfall. These gods need to be appeased in order to have plenty of rain for the rice crop. The celebration is also to remember a famous poet whose spirit is said to be in the river. Boat races are held,and special rice dumplings are thrown in the river. On each boat, a drummer is part of the crew to awaken the dragon gods and to keep the rowing synchronized. The dragon-shaped boats are 40 to 100 feet long with oars as long as 12 feet.

Preparation

To make the boats, each group will need:
- tin foil (about one foot long)
- clay
- toothpicks

You will need a water table or large tub of water.

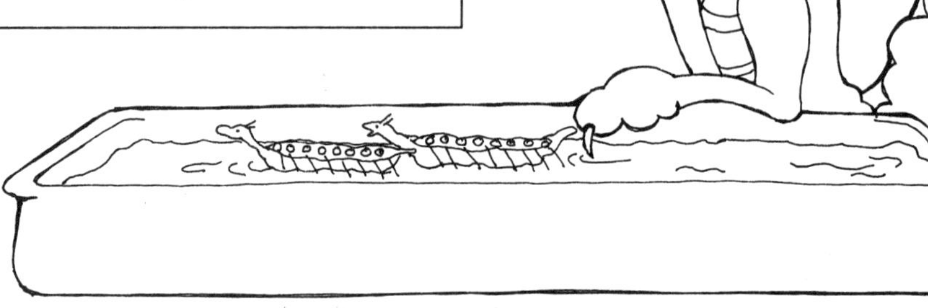

Activity

- Talk about the Dragon Boat Festival, and let the children figure out the length of the Chinese boats and oars by finding a comparable distance on the school grounds.
- Divide the children into groups of four.
- Have each group create a dragon boat out of tin foil.
- Encourage members of the group to make clay rowers to fill the boat. (Someone needs to create a drummer.) Toothpicks can be used as oars.
- Let the groups try their boats in the water. Ask questions such as, "How many rowers can your boat hold without sinking? Is there some way you can improve your boat to make it more seaworthy?"

Making Lanterns

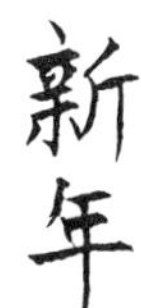

Cultural Background

Around January 15, on the first full moon of the year, the Chinese celebrate Lantern Festival Day as part of Sin Nian (Seen Nee-EHN), the New Year's festivities. Lanterns of all shapes, kinds and colors are displayed. Some lanterns are held on the ends of bamboo poles; others are displayed in doorways of shops and homes. Lanterns come in many shapes, such as animals, pagodas, cars, and fans. Some are mechanical. Others are made of blocks of ice or of glass!

Preparation

To make a lantern, each child will need:

- 4 small white paper plates

- 8 pieces of red yarn [(4 about 8" (20.5 cm) long, 4 about 12" (30.5 cm) long)]

- scissors, paste, hole punch, stapler

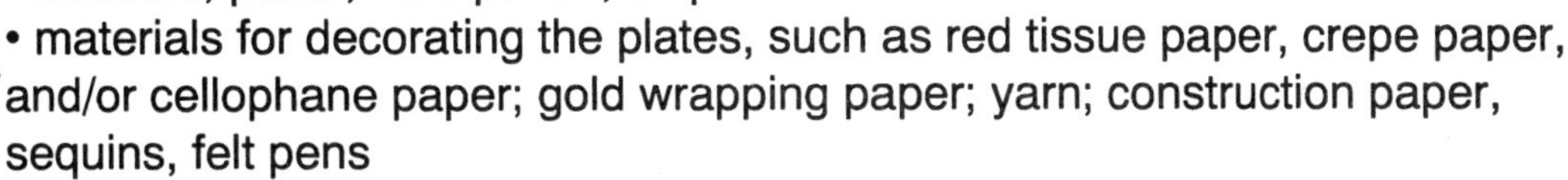

- materials for decorating the plates, such as red tissue paper, crepe paper, and/or cellophane paper; gold wrapping paper; yarn; construction paper, sequins, felt pens

You might want to find a cassette tape of Chinese music.

Activity

- To set the mood, you could play Chinese music in the background.
- Let each child decorate four small plates. Some ideas are as follows:
  - drawing with felt pens
  - writing Chinese characters (See pages 29-31.)
  - gluing on gold and red cut-outs, sequins, beads, yarn, etc.
  - punching holes and backing them with tissue or cellophane paper
  - making animal faces
- Staple the sides of the plates together as shown. Punch a hole on the top and bottom of each plate.
- Tie the yarn through the punched holes and hang in the windows.

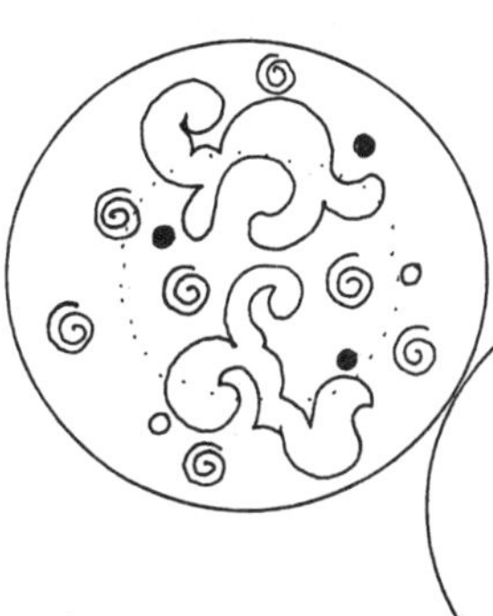

Cooking Won Ton

Cultural Background

The traditional food at the Dragon Boat Festival (see page 32) is called zhongzhi (ZTSUNG-zju). Zhongzhi is a rice dumpling wrapped in leaves (bamboo, palm or rice) and tied with a string. Inside could be such fillings as dates, walnuts, or beans. Zhongzhi is thrown overboard at the Dragon Boat Festival to feed the spirit of a famous poet said to be in the water. The recipe below is for won ton (wahn-TAHN), which are also considered dumplings, but are much easier to make than zhongzhi. Won ton means “cloud swallowing” because the won ton noodle looks like a cloud floating in the soup.

Preparation

To make won ton, you will need:	**You will need to:**
• 1 lb. pre-cooked ground meat • 2 T sugar • 2 T soy sauce • 2 T water • 2 T green onions • oil • about 60 won ton skins	• Divide the ingredients among four groups. • Give each group a copy of the instructions below. To eat with chopsticks, each child will need a copy of page 35.

Activity

• Have each group follow the instructions below:

• Talk about the geometric shapes (squares, triangles) in each step below:

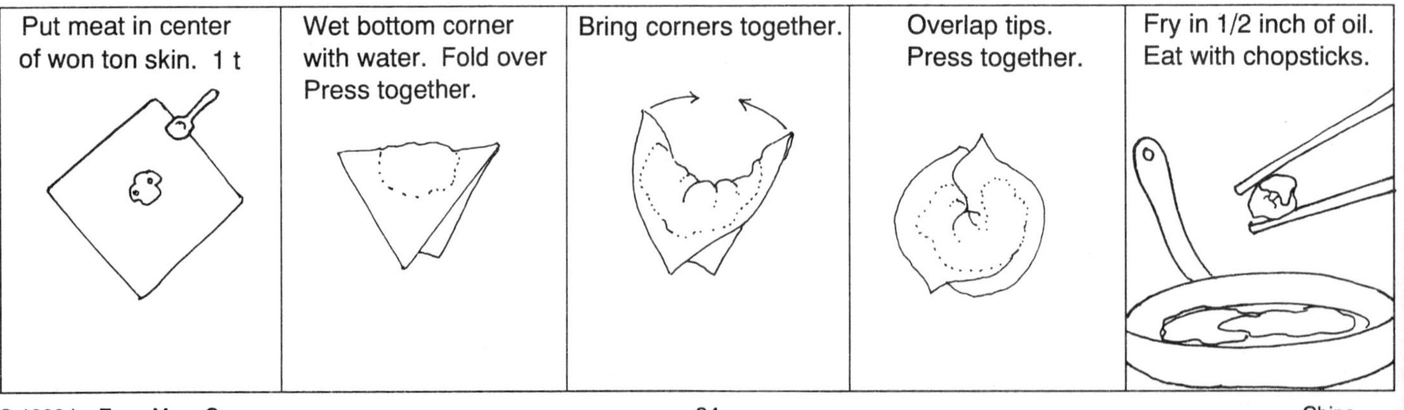

Using Chopsticks

1. Hold one chopstick like a pencil.

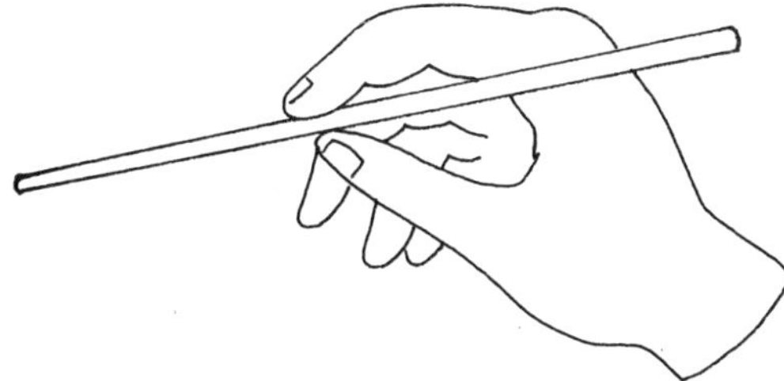

2. Slip the other chopstick in under the first one. Lean it against your third finger.

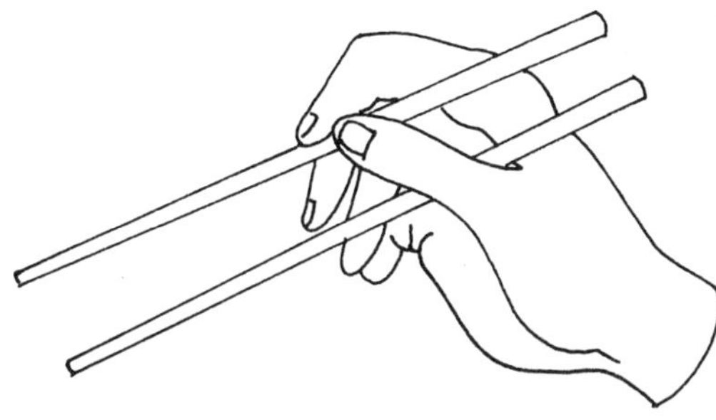

3. Move the second chopstick up and down to pick up food.

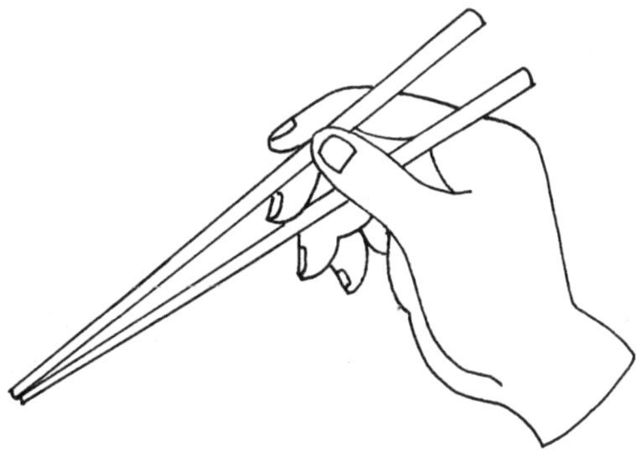

The easy way:

Wrap the chopsticks with a small piece of paper. Put a rubber band around the paper. Now try it!

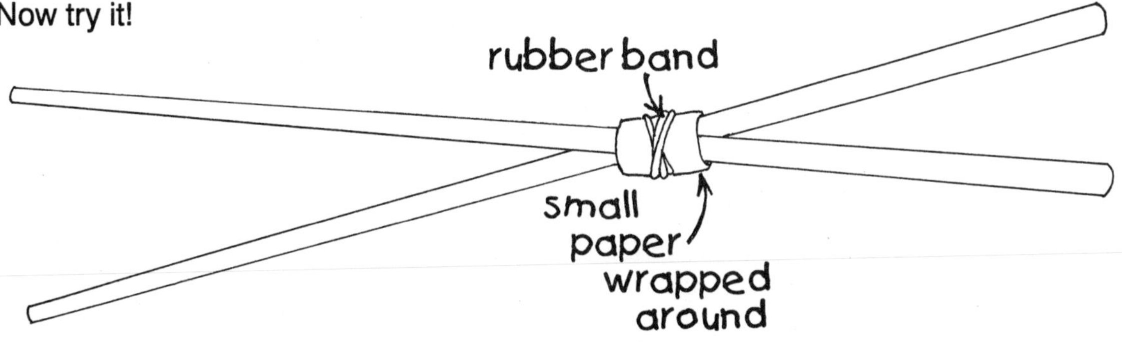

Math, Creative Arts, Social Studies

Making Red Envelopes

Cultural Background

On special occasions in a person's life and at celebrations, red envelopes containing money are given instead of a gift. The envelopes are given to sweeten a person's life and to bless them. Red is the traditional color of the envelopes because it signifies good luck. Envelopes are often decorated with Chinese characters and pictures, drawn in gold. Pairs are always preferable to single items in Chinese culture, so two envelopes are given at a time.

Preparation

To make 2 envelopes, each child will need:

- a copy of the form on page 37
- red, yellow, orange, and gold drawing materials (felt pens, crayons, and/or colored pencils)
- paste and scissors
- gold wrapping paper

You will need:

- play money

Activity

Making the Red Envelopes

- Have the children cut out the envelopes on their forms and fold them in half. Paste the envelopes shut.

- Encourage the children to decorate the the center of their envelopes with yellow, orange or gold. Then the rest of the envelope can be colored in red. Decorate the envelope with Chinese designs. Some samples are shown on page 37.

- Have gold wrapping paper available for children to paste to the envelopes.

Playing with the Red Envelopes

- Divide the children into groups of 4. Put a random amount of play money into each child's envelopes.
- Ask the group to figure out how much money they have altogether.
- Have the group figure out how to distribute the money equally among group members. This will lead to the necessity of exchanging their large coins for smaller coins. The group may find that the money cannot be divided evenly.

Red Envelopes continued

Raising Silkworms and Making Crickets

Cultural Background

Chinese children enjoy playing with and raising insects. Crickets are kept in bamboo cages, and beetles are collected in small boxes for trading. Even silkworms are raised from eggs to larva to pupa to adulthood.

Preparation

To simulate raising silkworms, each child will need:

- green paper leaves
- uncooked rice
- white pipe cleaners
- cotton balls
- bow tie noodles
- egg cartons
- cardboard boxes

To keep a silkworm journal, each child will need:

- a small booklet of at least four pages, in the shape of a moth.

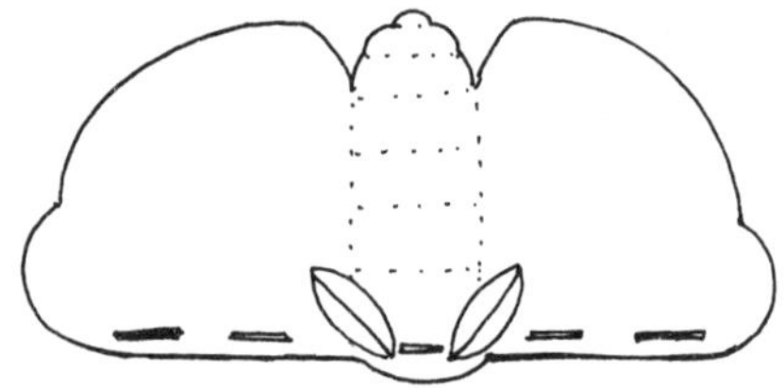

To raise silkworms, you will need:

- 25-30 silkworm eggs (Order from Carolina Biological Supply Co., 2700 York Rd., Burlington, North Carolina 27215)
- mulberry leaves
- egg cartons
- cardboard boxes
- magnifying glass

To make crickets, each child will need:

- clothespin
- green paint
- green construction-paper wings
- a small box/cage, paste, scissors

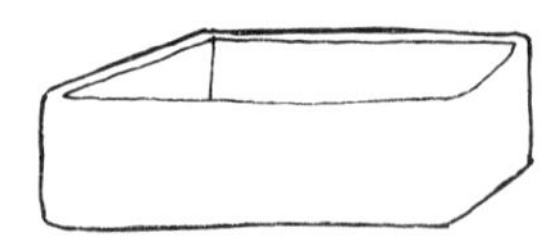

Activity

Raising Silkworms

- When mulberry leaves are available in the spring, order the silkworm eggs (2 day delivery). If mulberry leaves are not available, Carolina Biological Supply will also send silkworm food.
- Let the children use a magnifying glass to inspect the tiny eggs. They will hatch in 20 days.
- Provide ripped up dry leaves for the caterpillars (larva stage). Feed them for about 25 days, several times a day. Once a day, move the worms on the leaves to another box and clean the waste.
- When they move their heads and stop eating, put them in egg cartons.
- After 3 or 4 days, the pupa (cocoon) will form.
- After 3 weeks, the adults will emerge. They will mate and lay eggs. The eggs can be refrigerated until spring of the next year.

Simulating the Silkworm Cycle/Keeping Silkworm Journals

• Children can go through the cycle described above using green paper for leaves, rice for eggs, pipe cleaners for larva, cotton balls for pupa, and bow tie noodles for adults.
• They can put their display on a paper plate to show the cyclical nature of the stages.

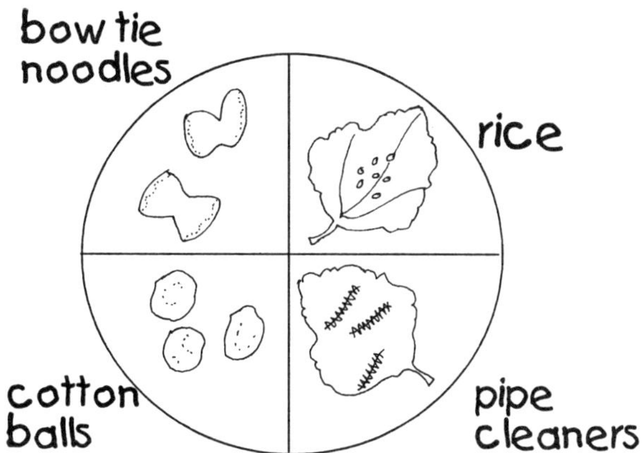

Keeping Silkworm Journals

• Have the children keep silkworm journals. Encourage them to pretend they are the insect at each stage. Help them dictate or write what each stage feels like: egg, larva, pupa, and adult.

Making Crickets

• Have the children paint their clothespins green.
• Let them cut out green wings to glue to their clothespin crickets.
• Keep the crickets in boxes, with leaves for food.
• If there are live crickets in your area, you could catch a few and keep them for a few days. Chinese children tickle them with feathers to make them move about.

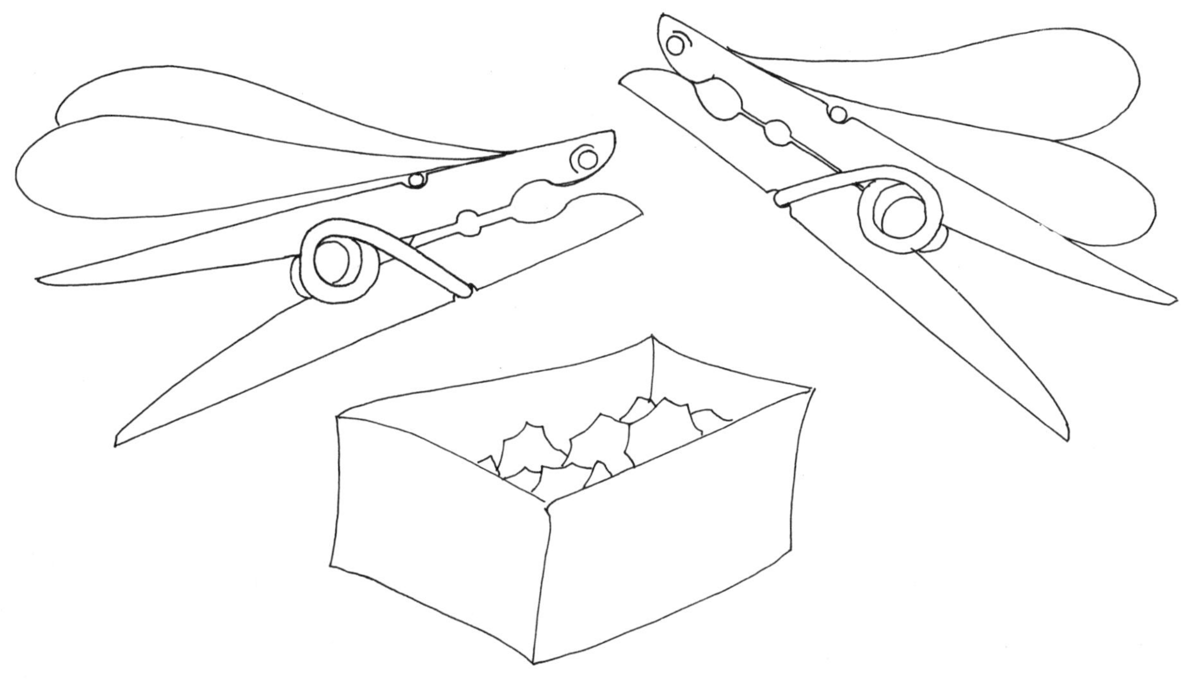

Doing Tai Ji Exercises

Cultural Background

Tai Ji (Tah-ee JEE) is sometimes called "Shadow Boxing." It is a silent, meditative art that is done by both adults and children in China. The moves, which are good for your health, also build strength for other forms of martial arts. Joints are always slightly bent, and breathing in and out is an important part of the exercises. All exercises are done very slowly.

Preparation

You might want to practice the stances and exercises before showing the children.

Activity

• Find out if any of your children take martial arts. This can lead into a discussion of Tai Ji.
• Practice the hand positions and stances with the children.

Hand Positions

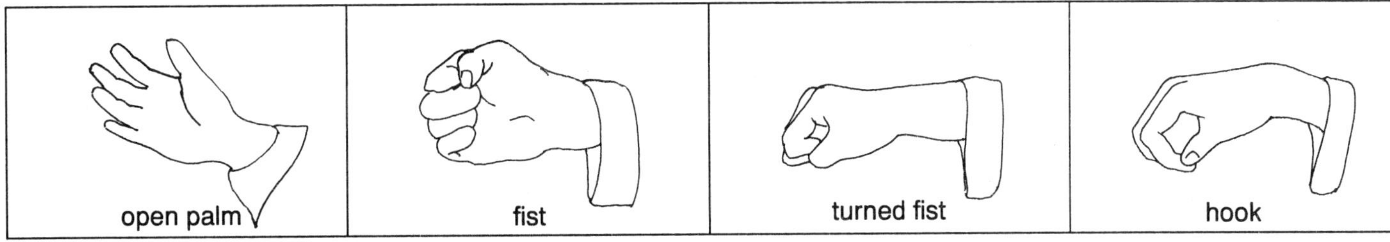

Stances

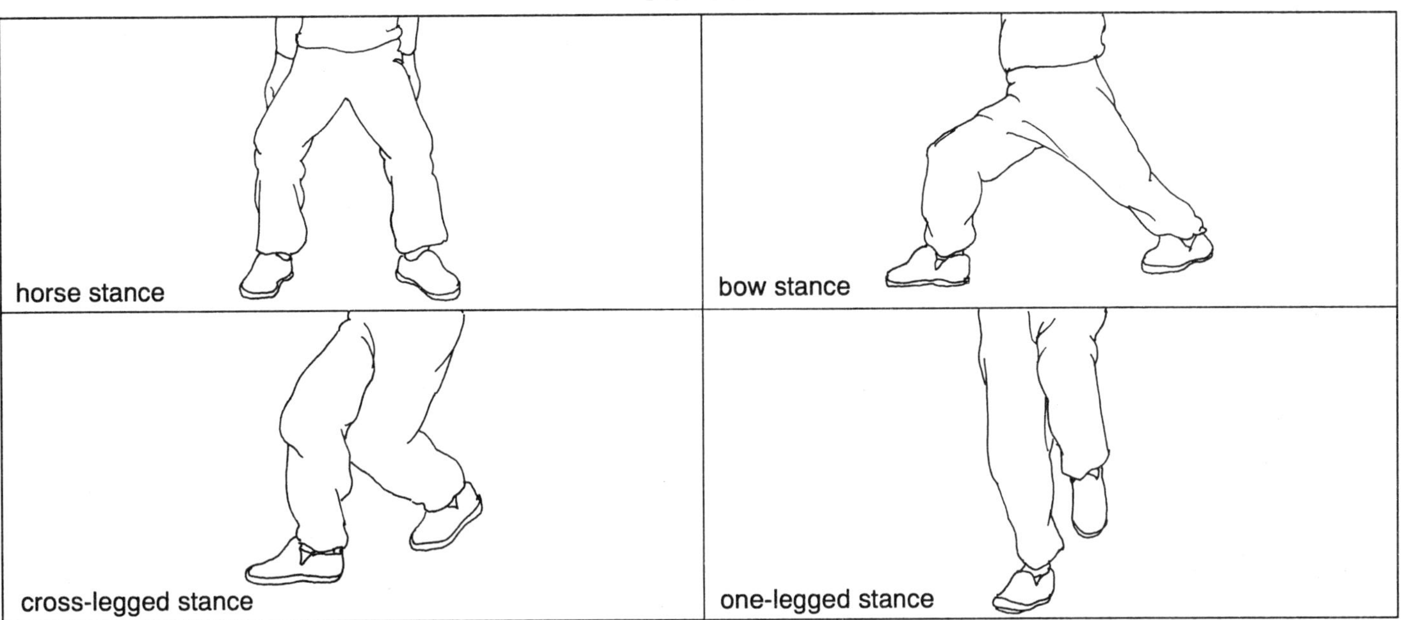

• Teach the children the exercise below:

Stroking Your Beard

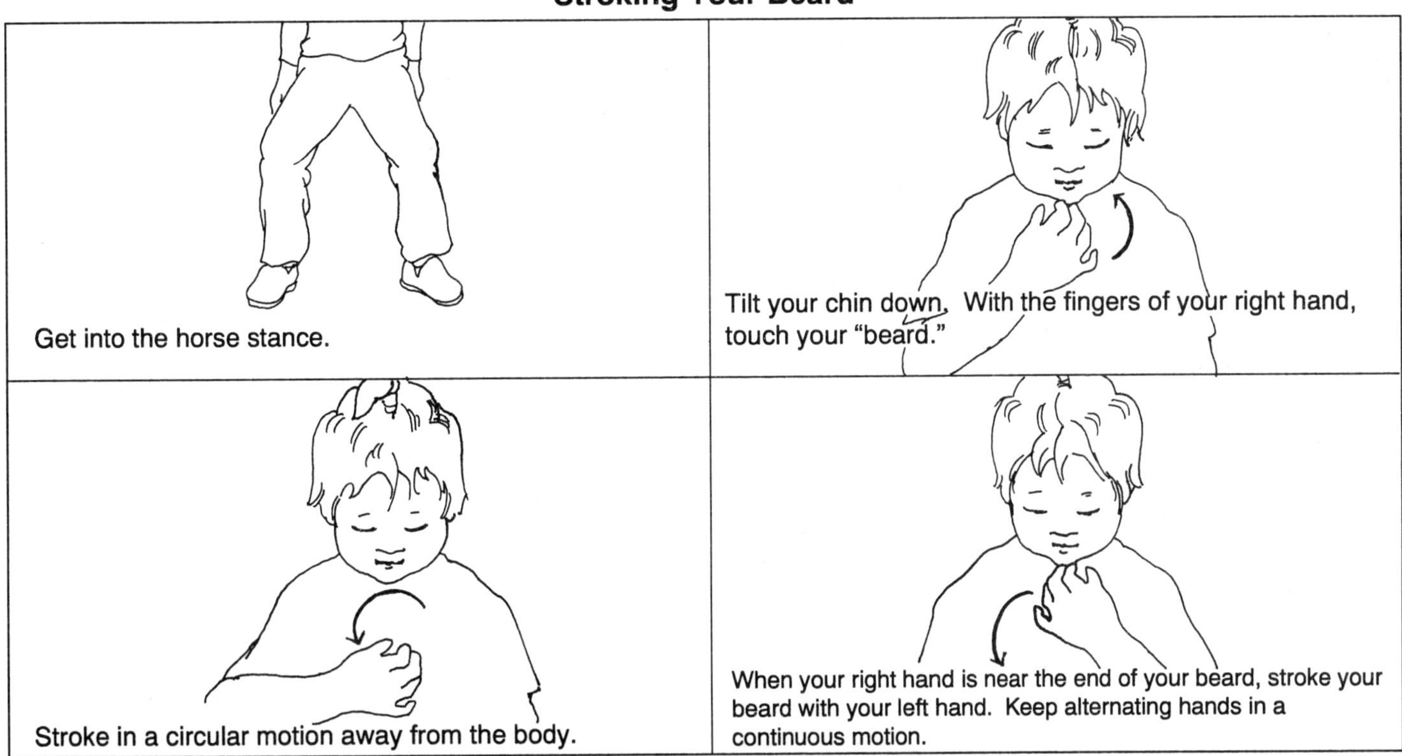

• The longer your beard, the wiser you are. Try the exercise with a longer and longer beard. (The longer the beard, the larger the circle the hands make.)

Playing Jump Rope

Cultural Background

Jump rope, or tiao siang chyuan (TEE-yoh see-AHNG chyoo-EHN), is a favorite pastime among Chinese children. Normally the rope is made of rubber bands looped together, giving it more elasticity. Sometimes children play with two ropes at one time. Sometimes they play very complicated games in which they manipulate two ropes with their feet. Their maneuvers resemble the moves in the string game, "Cat's Cradle." The game below involves jumping over a rope held between two people.

Preparation

To play the game, groups of children will need:
10 to 15 rubber bands.

Activity

Show the children how to loop the rubber bands together.

Game 1

- Two people hold the rope about 6 inches off the ground. Everyone jumps over it.
- The rope is raised higher and higher. Everyone tries to jump over it. Those who jump successfully over the rope remain in the game.

Game 2

- This game is the same as game 1 except that the players need to land on the rope with 2 feet, touch the ground, and jump off without losing their balance.
- The rope is raised after each round.

Game 3

- This time players land on the rope with one foot and jump off.

Playing a Game of Sticky Red Bean

Cultural Background

A special game of tag in China is called "Ji Hong Do" (Jee Hohn Doh). It means "Sticky Red Bean" in English. The game is played with an even number of players, with one of the players being "It." "It" tries to tag the other players. If a player is holding hands in a pair (or any even-numbered group of people), that player is safe. Players run around joining and leaving groups according to where "It" is.

Preparation

You might want to review the rules of the game before presenting them.

Activity

- Make sure there are an even number of children playing the game.
- Select one child to be "It."
- "It" tries to tag players out.
- Players are safe if they are in a pair (or in any other even-numbered group), holding hands.
- Players are unsafe if they are in an odd-numbered group, including by themselves.
- If a player joins an existing even-numbered group, someone else must leave the group. That player can always join another group.
- If a player is being chased, another player can come to his/her rescue by forming a pair.
- It's more fun if the children are brave and don't always stay in even groupings.

How to Use the Counting Chart

Use the Counting Chart on page 45 to acquaint children with how to count to ten in Chinese (Mandarin.) Leave the chart up in the classroom for the students to refer to while you are doing this unit on China.

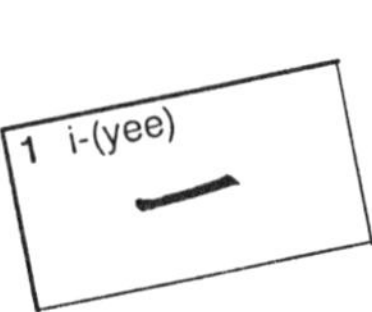

Counting Chart

1 i-(yee) 一	2 erh-(ur) 二
3 san-(sahn) 三	4 ssu-(shu) 四
5 wu-(woh) 五	6 liu-(LYEE-ooh) 六
7 chi-(chee) 七	8 pa-(bah) 八
9 chiu-(jyee-OH) 九	10 shih-(sshu) 十

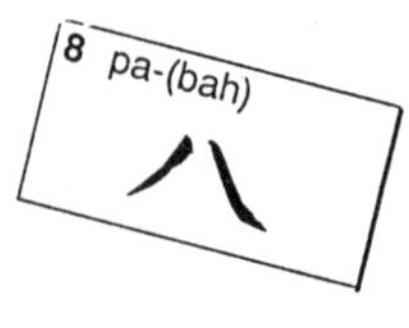

1. Provide students with many opportunities to count in Chinese.

2. Allow students a chance to go to a paint center and practice writing the Chinese characters for the numbers.

3. Students may enjoy creating a counting book with Chinese characters and words. Each page of the book could be a different number and the pictures could be of typically Chinese things.

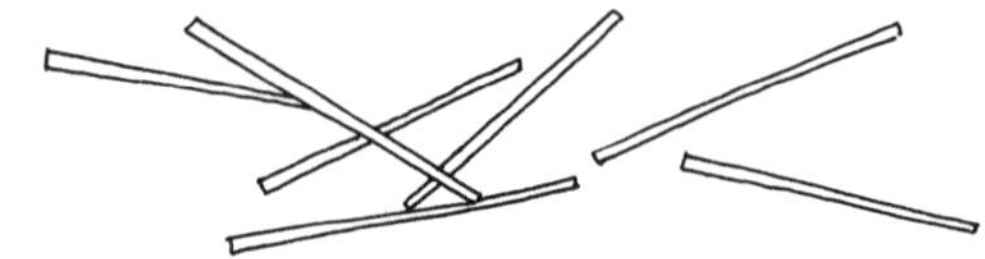

4. Make a copy of the Counting Chart. Cut the numbers apart and let the students sequence the numerals as they count.

Counting Chart

1 i-(yee) 一	**2** erh-(ur) 二
3 san-(sahn) 三	**4** ssu-(shu) 四
5 wu-(woh) 五	**6** liu-(LYEE-ooh) 六
7 chi-(chee) 七	**8** ba-(bah) 八
9 chiu-(jyee-OH) 九	**10** shih-(sshu) 十

The Chinese Flags

Here are the flags of two Chinas!

Mainland China is a gigantic 3,700,000 square miles with a population of over a billion.

The flag of mainland China is red with yellow stars.

Taiwan is an island off the southeastern coast of Mainland China with an area of only 14,000 square miles but a population of around 25 million.

The corner of the flag is blue with a white circle and triangles. The rest of the flag is red.

These two Chinas formed separate governments after World War II.

Map of China

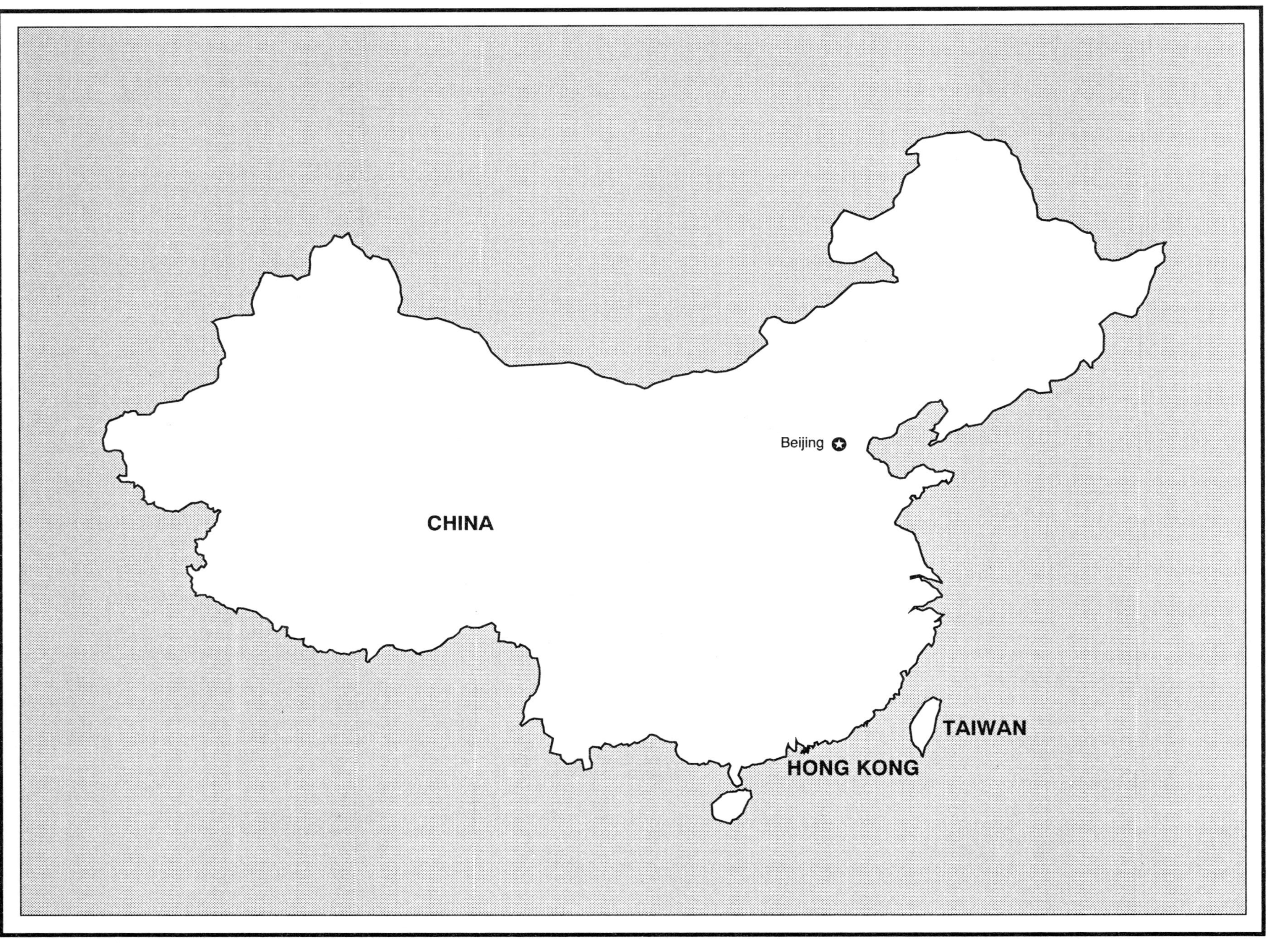

Glossary

da (dah) — big
Duan Wu Jie (Dwahn Woh JEE-eh) — the Dragon Boat Festival
fan (fahn) — cooked rice
hsia (shyah) — below
ji hong do (jee hohn doh) — sticky bean
lyong (lyohng) — dragon
ma (mah, falling and rising tone) — horse
ma (mah, flat tone) — mother
Ni hao ma (nee how mah) — How are you?
shang (shahng) — above
Sin Nian (Seen Nee-EHN) — New Year's
Tai Ji (tah-ee JEE) — a meditative art, consisting of precise slow movements of the body; practiced to promote health and to build strength for other martial arts
tai yiang (tah-ee yohng) — sun
tiao siang chyuan (TEE-yoh see-AHNG chyoo-EHN) — jump rope
won ton (wahn TAHN) — a Chinese dumpling consisting of a noodle stuffed with meat and/or vegetables; means "cloud swallowing"
zhongzhi (ZTSUNG-zju) — a traditional rice dumpling made at the time of the Dragon Boat Festival; wrapped in leaves, tied with a string, and stuffed with such treats as walnuts, beans, and dates
(All words except *won ton* are in Mandarin Chinese.)

Additional Resources

A Chinese Zoo: Fables and Proverbs by Demi; Harcourt Brace Jovanovich, 1987
Dragon Kites and Dragonflies by Demi; Harcourt Brace Jovanovich, 1986
Liang and the Magic Paintbrush by Demi; Holt, Rinehart, and Winston, 1980
The Empty Pot by Demi; Henry Holt & Co., 1990
The Magic Boat by Demi; Henry Holt & Co., 1990
Under the Shade of the Mulberry Tree by Demi; Prentice-Hall, 1979
The Story About Ping by Marjorie Flack; Weston Woods, 1933
A Family in China by Nance Lui Fyson, and Richard Greenhill; Lerner Publications Company, 1985
Mei Li by Thomas Handforth; Doubleday, 1938
The Weaving of a Dream by Marilee Heyer; Viking Kestrel, 1986
How the Ox Star Fell from Heaven by Lily Toy Hong; Albert Whitman, 1991
Silkworms by Sylvia A. Johnson; Lerner Publishing Co., 1982
Eyes of the Dragon by Margaret Leaf; Lothrop, Lee & Shepard Books, 1987
Ming Lo Moves the Mountain by Arnold Lobel; Scholastic, Inc., 1982
Yeh-Sheh by Ai-Ling Louie; Philomel Books, 1982
The Seven Chinese Brothers by Margaret Mahy; Scholastic, Inc., 1990
Take a Trip to China by Sally Mason; Franklin Watts, 1981
Tikki Tikki Tembo by Arlene Mosel; Scholastic, Inc., 1968
A Grain of Rice by Helena Clare Pittman; Kampmann & Co., 1986
The Moon Lady by Amy Tan; Macmillan Pub. Co., 1992
The Rat, the Ox, and the Zodiac by Dorothy Van Woerkom; Crown Publishers, 1976
Everyone Knows What a Dragon Looks Like by Jay Williams; Four Winds Press, 1976
8,000 Stones by Diane Wolkstein; Doubleday, 1972
The Jade Stone by Caryn Yacowitz; Holiday House, 1992
The Seeing Stick by Jane Yolen; Crowell, 1977
Lon Po Po by Ed Young; Philomel Books, 1989
The Terrible Nung Gwama by Ed Young; Collins/World, 1978
China, Here We Come by Tang Yungmei; G.P. Putnam's Sons, 1981